GREAT WESTERN STEAM IN ACTION 7

L. M. COLLINS

D. BRADFORD BARTON LIMITED

Frontispiece: 'Castle' No.5083 *Bath Abbey* has arrived at Hereford heading an express from Paddington as 'Manor' No.7808 *Cookham Manor* rolls in with a stopping passenger train from South Wales; 25 June 1957.
[R. K. Evans]

© copyright D. Bradford Barton 1978   *784/2 PN*   *IRRC*   *ISBN 0 85153 334 5*

printed in Great Britain by H. E. Warne Ltd, London and St. Austell

for the publishers

D. BRADFORD BARTON LTD · Trethellan House · Truro · Cornwall · England

introduction

We all have some favourite memory of the Great Western from years gone by: a 'King' storming through Sonning cutting at the head of a 14 coach West of England express; perhaps a 45xx tank with a two coach set in the leafy depths of the Forest of Dean; a 28xx slogging freight up the climb into Birmingham (Snow Hill); a 'Castle' on the 'Torbay Express' sweeping along the superb Devon coastline past Teignmouth; or, at the other end of the scale, an ageing pannier tank simmering quietly in the intervals between shunting on some now-forgotten branch line. All these scenes, once commonplace, can now only be memories, or be recalled for us in photographs. Almost a decade has passed since steam passed away on the Western Region in 1965 and the rising generation has known, at first hand, none of the above. They can travel on the Dart and Severn Valley lines or elsewhere, it is true, but these recapture only a part of steam as it once was.

The opportunity has been taken in this seventh volume in

the series—the thirty-third in the Great Western Steam series as a whole—to include a proportion of scenes from some less familiar byways, on the once quite busy network of minor lines in Shropshire, Worcestershire and Herefordshire. As before, the overall aim is to present a representative cross-section of ex-G.W.R. steam at work across the system; that one is able to do so without repetition—except of the occasional location which by reason of its setting or variety of traffic warrants it—is a tribute not only to the photographers whose lineside work we see here but also to the G.W.R. as a system without equal . . . .

Further volumes are planned as sequels to this one; those who remember the G.W.R. with affection and have photographs of suitable quality may be interested to make these available for possible inclusion. The grateful thanks of editor and publisher are recorded here to those who have contributed photographs and/or information herein, as well as in the other volumes in the series.

No.7031 *Cromwell's Castle* in a familiar setting at the exit from Paddington picks up speed with a down express in August 1962—a photograph taken from beside Ranelagh Bridge locomotive yard.

[T. E. Williams]

Signs of the impending change to diesels on Western Region, with No.4089 *Donnington Castle* barely able to get into one of the layover roads at Ranelagh Bridge yard as a result of fuel tank wagons needed for the new diesel motive power coming into service. Behind is 'Hymek' Class 35 No.D7033. Note the very extensive pointwork beneath the bridge to enable locomotives coming into or out of the yard to run to or from any of Paddington's platform lines.

[T. E. Williams]

The young fireman of 2-6-2T No.6158 has just hosed down the footplate during a stop at Southall with an up local bound for Paddington, 18 April 1960.

[A. Tyson]

No.7005 *Lamphey Castle* between Langley and Iver with an up express from Hereford and Worcester, 24 April 1957.   Below, another 'Castle', No.5042 *Winchester Castle*, approaching Iver on the down fast line with a parcels train for Fishguard on the same day.

[A. R. Butcher]

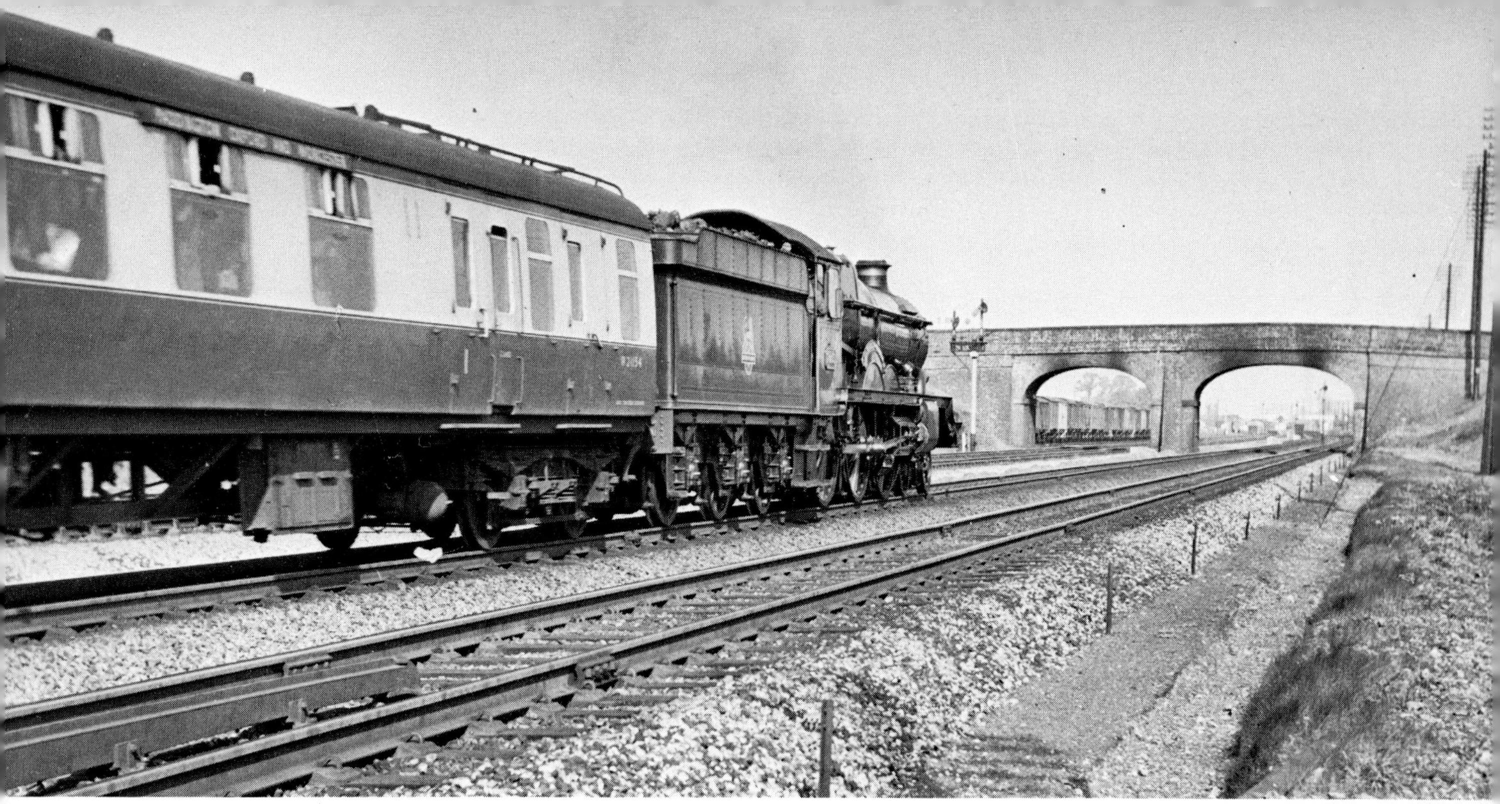

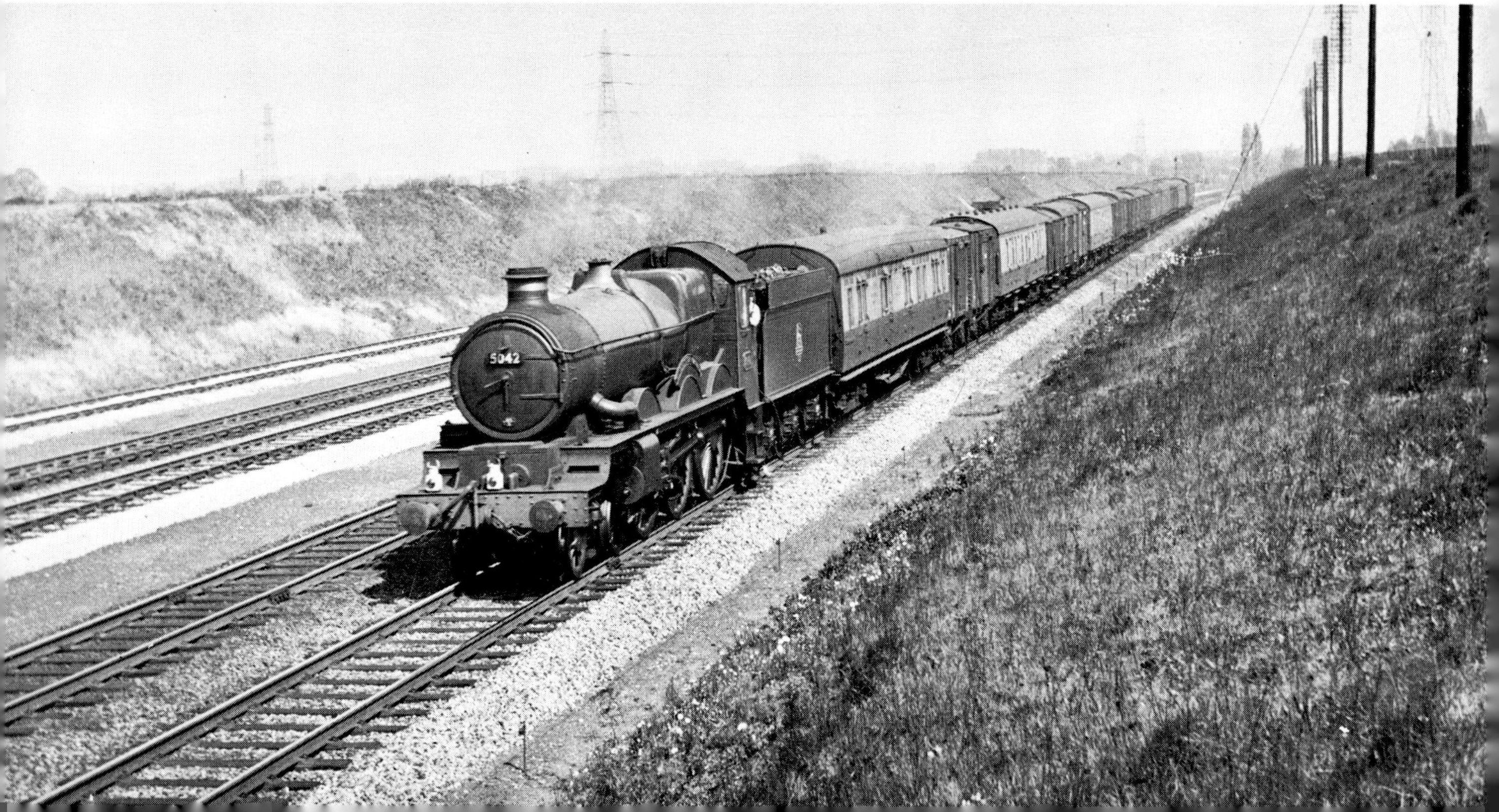
5042

No.6811 *Cranbourne Grange* piloting No.5982 *Harrington Hall* with an easily-managed eight coach load forming a Frome-Paddington train on 11 October 1958, near Twyford. With one engine well kept and the other one far from clean, they almost appear to be in different liveries.　　　　[T. E. Williams]

The principal bridge over Sonning Cutting carries the A4 main road and here forms a setting for No.5929 *Hanham Hall,* plodding west with empty coal wagons bound for South Wales.

[F. Robinson]

No.5982 *Harrington Hall* has a clear road for the run to Paddington, with both boards off for the up main out of Reading.

[C. J. Blay]

A close-up of Mogul No.7331 at Reading, with her grizzled veteran of a driver looking back for any signs of trouble.
[C. J.Blay]

No.6013 *King Henry VIII* with a 14-coach load on the down 'Limited' slows for an adverse signal near Reading West on 29 June 1957. Her crew are probably cursing some slower train which is running just ahead of them.   [L. Elsey]

Upper quadrant signals betray 'foreign' territory—2-8-0 No.2883 trundling past Salisbury 'C' box with a short freight from Westbury on 22 January 1962. To the left is the SR motive power depot.   [G. A. Richardson]

Two views of the 5.02 p.m. to Cardiff, about to depart from Salisbury on 25 July 1951 behind 'Saint' class No.2950 *Taplow Court.*

[R. K. Evans]

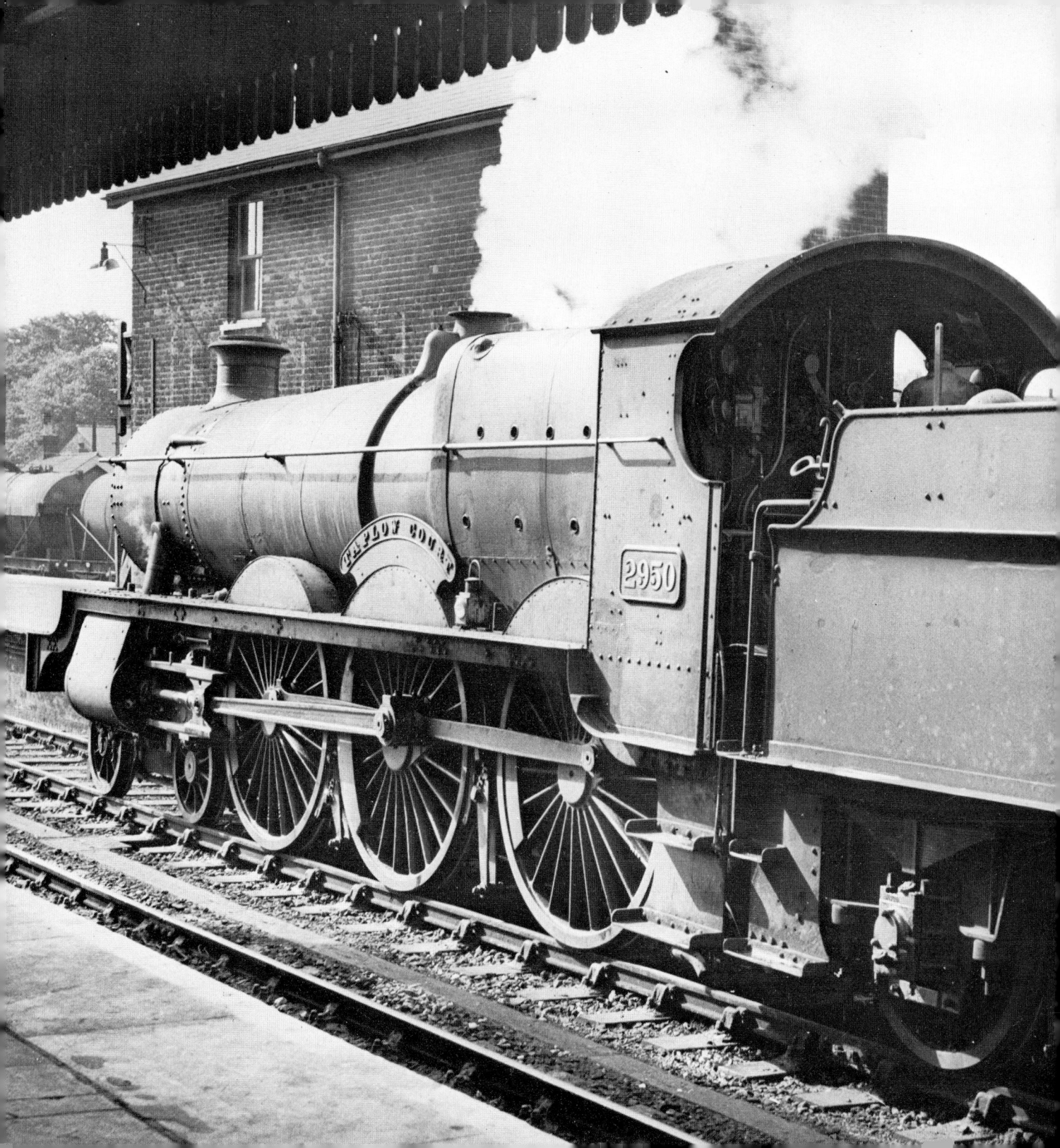

One of the big 47xx 2-8-0s was involved in a triple collision at Highworth Junction, east of Swindon, on the night of 11/12 November 1958 when she over-ran the end of the goods loop at the head of a Bristol-Reading freight. A second freight, from Fishguard to Paddington, ran into some of the de-railed wagons and this was followed by the down Carmarthen newspaper train colliding with the wreckage. Although no-one was injured, the wreckage was quite spectacular and took some clearing up.

[T. E. Williams]

Breakdown cranes about to make a start on lifting 2-8-0 No. 4707—a 75-ton lift and at an awkward distance—after the Highworth Junction accident in November 1958.

[R. C. H. Nash]

'Kings' at the Races; No.6025 *King Henry III* and No.6000 *King George V* at Newbury
Racecourse platforms; both are in double chimney form.   [D. Bullock]

2-8-0 No.4706 pulls into the goods loop at Foxhall Junction, Didcot, with a down mixed freight on 17 August 1960. On some of the longer distance overnight freights worked by the 47xxs, firing was a job second only to that on a 'King'.
[T. E. Williams]

No.5969 *Honington Hall* hurries a three-coach express over Aynho troughs on 16 June 1960.
[Rev. A. C. Cawston]

No.5916 *Trinity Hall* approaching Kings Sutton with a three-coach train of compartment stock and an SR van in April 1962.   [T. E. Williams]

The driver of 51xx class 2-6-2T No.4112 has just seen that he is signalled into the goods loop at Fosse Road, near Leamington Spa, and has closed the regulator smartly, ready to slow his freight to the permitted speed; 5 March 1960.   [T. E. Williams]

No.5936 *Oakley Hall* has the Stratford-on-Avon banker, 0-6-0 No.2203, coupled inside the train engine, with a Paignton-Wolverhampton train, 23 August 1952. The setting is the top of Wilmcote bank, where the 1 in 75 north of Stratford faced trains bound for the Midlands.

[T. E. Williams]

In the 1950s, one of the favourite turns of the two remaining 'Stars' at Stafford Road shed was this mid-day Wolverhampton-Paddington stopping train known locally as the 'up cheap'; No.4061 *Glastonbury Abbey* on 20 February 1954 takes water on Rowington troughs, near Lapworth, on this service.

[T. E. Williams]

Hawksworth's ten 1500 class 0-6-0 pannier tanks had a great deal of useful life left in them when they began to be displaced by diesels and three of them were sold to the National Coal Board—one in 1959 and two in 1961. One of the latter pair was No.1502, seen here with spark-arrester at Coventry Colliery in August 1969 *en route* to the BR exchange sidings at Bedworth to pick up coal empties. No.1501 went to the Severn Valley Railway but the other two (including No.1502) were scrapped in 1970. [V. C. K. Allan]

No.6999 *Capel Dewi Hall,* from Cardiff (Canton), running down grade through Earlswood on the North Warwickshire line with the 3.45 p.m. Birmingham (Snow Hill)-Fishguard train on 2 August 1958. [T. E. Williams]

Another well-kept 'Castle', on this occasion No.5076 *Gladiator* from Reading shed, going well through Honeybourne ready for the start of the 1 in 100 climb for four miles up to Campden tunnel with a Sunday morning Worcester-Paddington train.

[T. E. Williams]

A classic study of one of Worcester's 'Castles'—No.7005 *Sir Edward Elgar*—heading the up 'Cathedrals Express' between Honeybourne and Chipping-Campden; 24 June 1961.

[T. E. Williams]

It was rare that South Wales-Paddington trains were diverted via Leamington and Banbury but in May 1959 the derailment of the up 'Pembroke Coast Express' near Slough caused this and was responsible for this scene of No.7012 *Barry Castle* leaving Harbury Tunnel with the 7.45 a.m. Cardiff-Paddington relief.
[T. E. Williams]

0-6-0PT No.4645 showing her capabilities in no uncertain fashion with a quite lengthy freight from off the Bala line, passing the signal box controlling Cefn (or Llangollen) Junction near Ruabon in March 1962.

[A. Tyson]

2-6-2T No.4120 with a Crewe-Wellington train at Market Drayton on 4 August 1959. This GWR line joined the LMS (ex-LNWR) line near Nantwich with the GWR/LMSR joint line at Wellington and also connected at Market Drayton with the LMS (ex North Staffordshire) line. [P. J. Shoesmith]

Moguls did great work on the long wandering line to Bala and Barmouth and No.7310 from Croes Newydd shed was one of its regulars. Ahead from this stop at Llangollen she has a couple of miles of 1 in 110 and 1 in 80 up the valley to Deeside Tunnel and the severe curve of the platforms seen here show how a constant succession of these up the valley will add to the power needed to work the train. From here onwards, it is single line for the fifty-mile run to the coast at Barmouth.

[A. Tyson]

Another Mogul, No.6339, departing from Dolgelly—today Dolgellau—with a train to Ruabon. In the inland (up) direction there is a more severe climb than the longer run from Llangollen, with a ten mile climb from Dolgelly on gradients as severe as 1 in 50. Oh! for a week in that Camping Coach in the siding watching Moguls, 'Manors' and Prairies coming and going.

[A. Tyson]

Exchanging the token at Morfa Mawddach; No.5399 leaving for Barmouth in August 1961. The south end of the viaduct across the estuary is visible in front of the locomotive.   [A. Tyson]

No.7821 *Ditcheat Manor* brings her three-coach train from Dovey Junction off the long viaduct at Barmouth on a day in May 1962. With clear weather, the Cader Idris range on the other side of the Mawddach estuary forms a striking backdrop. Just visible in the foreground, crossing under the line, is the short broad gauge 'railway' used to launch Barmouth lifeboat. [M. J. Messenger]

Class 4 No.75004 with a freight leaving Morfa Mawddach on 18 May 1966—on what was said to be the last steam working over the coast line. These 4-6-0s were Swindon-built from 1951 to 1957, with double blastpipe and chimney; they were virtually a light Class 5 with 17½-ton axle load, being very comparable to the Class 4 2-6-4 tank but with the longer range of a tender engine as was desirable on several routes in Wales.   [C. J. Blay]

One of the postwar BR Standard Moguls, No.46519 has the miniature 'Engineers Inspection' decorated headboard on its smokebox at Barmouth on 26 May 1961, on a tour of inspection of the Coast Line.
[M. J. Messenger]   47

At Moat Lane Junction the line to Builth Wells (seen here on the right) joined the main Shrewsbury-Aberystwyth line and this rural junction in mid Wales remained strongly Cambrian or GWR in character right to the early 1960s. This scene on 22 May 1959 shows No.7819 *Hinton Manor* taking water with an Aberystwyth-Welshpool train.

[M. J. Jackson]

Looking the other way at Moat Lane along the main line toward Aberystwyth, with the same train drawing in shortly before. The junction here was the sole *raison d'être* for the station, for there was no town or village to be served, as was also the case at Bala Junction on the Ruabon-Barmouth line.

[M. J. Jackson]

An afternoon train from Much Wenlock to Wellington crossing the River Severn between Buildwas and Coalbrookdale on 25 July 1959, headed by 2-6-2T No.4158. [P. J. Shoesmith]

Veteran 'Dean Goods' No.2516 at weed-grown and almost derelict Kerry station in the heart of Montgomeryshire in 1955. This short branch, which left the ex-Cambrian main line at Abermule, had a m.p.h. speed restriction over it—lower than virtually any other GWR branch on the system. It was closed the following summer. No.2516 is now preserved in Swindon Museum. [G. F. Bannister]

Pannier tank No.3782 by Sutton Bridge Junction signal box at Shrewsbury, engaged in shunting. In the background is the joint ex-GW/LMSR running shed. [T. E. Williams]

A three-coach Gloucester to Hereford train entering Ross-on-Wye behind Mogul No.6365, July 1964.
[P. Cookson]

Overleaf: Mogul No.6304 prepares to leave Ross-on-Wye with the 2.35 p.m. Hereford-Gloucester on 28 August 1962, photographed from the 2.08 from Gloucester. [W. L. Underhay]

The Hereford-Gloucester passenger services were usually in the hands of either Churchward Moguls or large Prairies. Here 2-6-0 No.7318 enters Grange Court Junction in the summer of 1964, bound for Gloucester.

[P. Cookson]

A Saturday excursion bound for Aberavon (Seaside) in July 1962 leaving Treherbert at the head of the Western Valleys behind 2-6-2T No.4144. This train would run over the line of the former Rhondda and Swansea Bay Railway, which connected with the Taff Vale at Treherbert and was taken over by the GWR in 1922. The main feature was the Treherbert (or Blaen-Rhondda) Tunnel, no less than 1 mile 168 yards long, which carried the line westward out of the upper Rhondda Valley near Treherbert.

[P. Cookson]

One of the hard-working 56xx tanks being flogged up the bank towards Stormy Down on the South Wales main line approaching Pyle station with an up freight.

[S. Rickard]

West Wales never received the same attention from lineside photographers as did most other parts of the ex-GWR system, particularly so compared to South-Western England. Carmarthen was always something of a frontier post, despite some good scenic locations farther west. This scene is of Mogul No.7340 at Carmarthen station on 24 June 1961, in ex-works condition.

[A. Tyson]

57xx 0-6-0PT No.9675 waits in the snow at Talybont-on-Usk for a Newport-Brecon train to pass; 29 December 1962.   [John Goss]

Traffic in iron ore from the north Oxfordshire deposits near Banbury gave rise to a constant string of loaded trains to the South Wales steel works, and empties back again. In this scene, 2-8-0 No.2895 heads a rake of empties from Rogerstone to Honeybourne, photographed near Penpergwm (south of Abergavenny) on 24 May 1958.

[R. K. Taylor]

2-6-2T No.6140 shunting at Ledbury on a pick-up freight turn, April 1964. Ledbury in steam days saw considerable through traffic, being at the meeting place of lines connecting Hereford, Worcester and Gloucester.

[Derek Cross]

0-6-0PT No.1616, with spark arrester fitment on the chimney, running light off the line from Ledbury at Over Junction, outside Gloucester.

[M. J. Jackson]

An unusual scene at Over Junction, with 0-6-0 No.2295 on the 8 a.m. Hereford-Gloucester pick-up freight coupled ahead of the 9.45 a.m. Alexander Dock Junction (Newport)-Stourbridge freight, headed by a Mogul on 12 February 1958. They are being worked together over the short but busy section from here through Gloucester Central.

[M. J. Jackson]

Collett 0-6-0 No.2242 at Tramway Junction, Gloucester, in April 1965.

[Derek Cross]

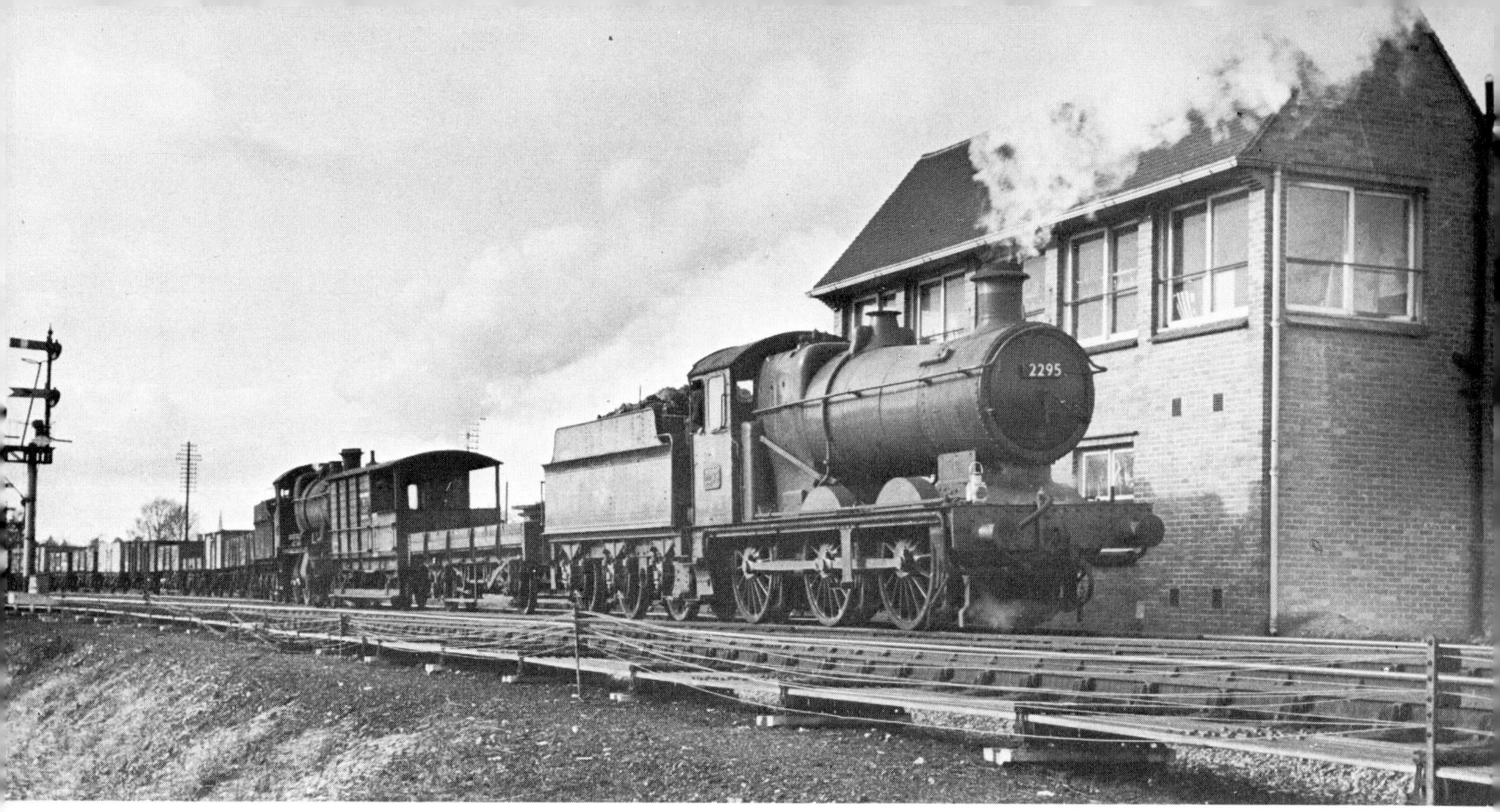
2295

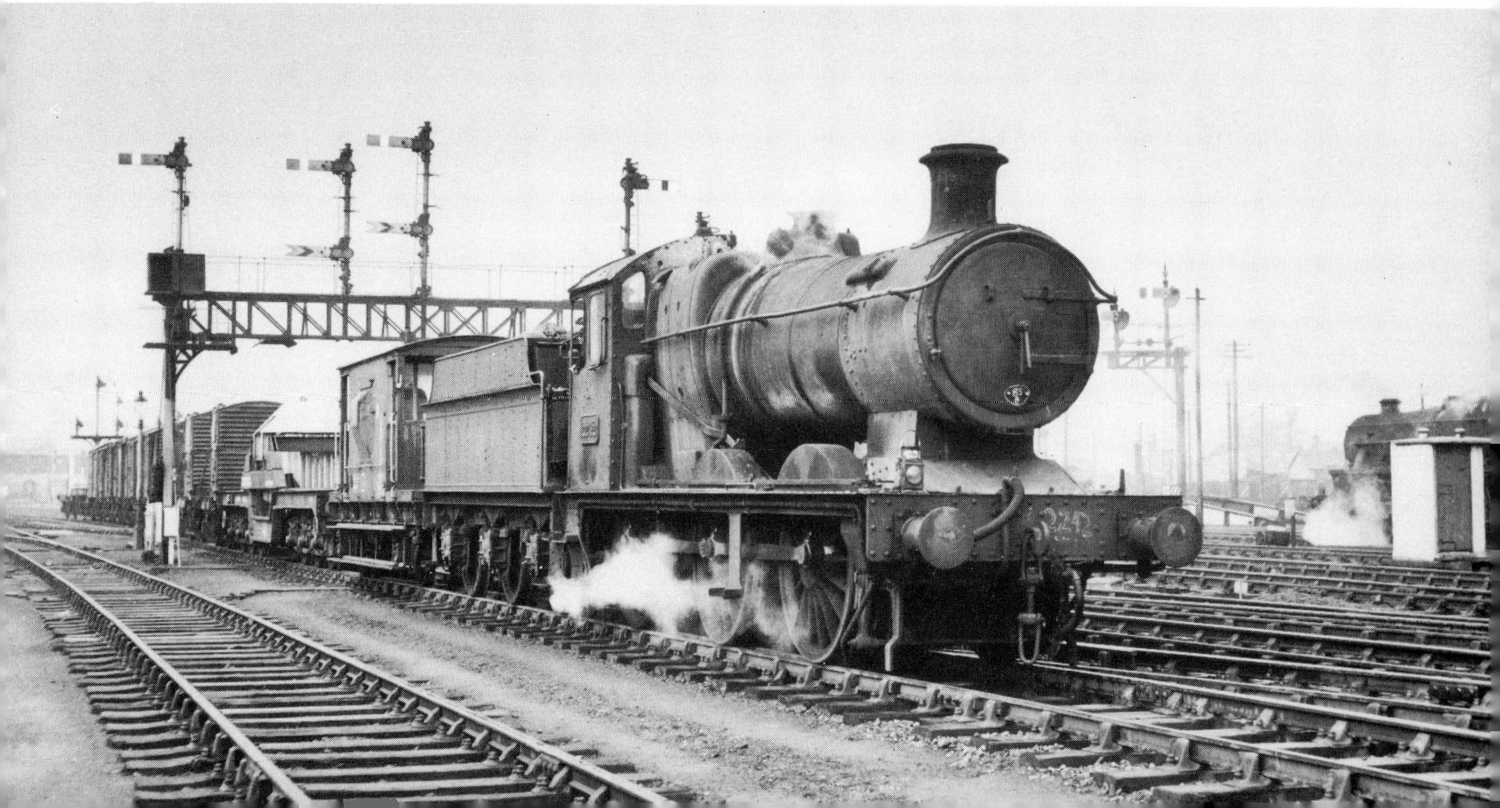

A long string of empty iron-ore tipplers trail behind No.5990 *Dorford Hall,* north-bound near Cheltenham, 10 June 1964.   [Derek Cross]

At Lansdown Junction, south of Cheltenham, the two pairs of ex-LMSR and ex-GWR lines which run side by side from here to south of Gloucester, part company. The ex-LMSR tracks, seen on the left below, head for Bromsgrove and Birmingham; the ex-GWR tracks, on the right, for Cheltenham, Honeybourne and the Midlands. 0-6-0PT No.9471 is heading a Cheltenham-Paddington train towards Gloucester, where a 'Castle' will take over; June 1964.   [Derek Cross]

Another Paddington express, this time a down working, near Churchdown (two miles or so north of Gloucester) heading for Cheltenham behind 0-6-2T No.6696. As usual, this train has reversed at Gloucester and left the large locomotive there; 29 July 1961. Nowhere else on the GWR system was it customary to see small tank engines regularly working main line expresses. [T. E. Williams]

A scene near Tuffley Junction, south of the network of lines at Gloucester, with 2-6-0 No.7338 heading a varied assortment of stock making up the 8.48 a.m. Fishguard to Paddington parcels on 17 June 1960, running late after a derailment on the South Wales main line. In the foreground are the ex-LMSR Birmingham-Bristol lines. [M. J. Jackson]

Helped in the rear by the 51xx 2-6-2T banker from Brimscombe, No.6838 *Goodmoor Grange* tackles the stiff climb up Sapperton bank with a heavy ballast train. With gradients up to 1 in 60 for the last half mile before the summit tunnel, this was a severe climb, extending some seven miles in all from Stroud. Officially this was termed the Brimscombe Incline in GWR service timetables.   [John Goss]

Another lineside photographer recorded No.6838 on a day of rain in July 1963—this time fresh out of Swindon Works after overhaul. She is in the approach cutting to the tunnel entrance and still with a mile of uphill work ahead. Out of sight in the rear is the usual 2-6-2T 'helper'.   [R. H. Leslie]

Two views of a p.w. maintenance train from Swindon on a Sunday in April 1953 engaged on turning the rails of the up line near Sapperton—a method of counteracting the uneven wear these receive on severe curves, and thus extending their useful life. Over these reverse curves, down trains were restricted to 40 m.p.h. maximum speed (and unfitted freights to 20 m.p.h.) whilst even up trains, working against the gradient, had a normal speed limit of 50 m.p.h. permanently in force.

[P. Q. Treloar]

0-6-0PT No.3601, with 'gig', shunting at Kidderminster on 14 April 1957.   [N. E. Preedy collection]

0-6-0PT No.4698 pounds up the 1 in 31 gradient on the Coleford branch in the heart of
the Forest of Dean with empty 'Herrings' for Whitecliff Quarry on 18 August 1965.
[R. Fisher]

Pannier tank No.8741 makes an attractive sight framed under the typical GWR footbridge at Hallatrow
station, heading the 2.53 p.m. Bristol-Frome on 12 September 1959. [D. H. Ballantyne]

0-4-2T No.1462 on duty as yard pilot at Swindon Works, 17 September 1958. To see a 14xx on other than branch line work was always somewhat unusual. [M. J. Jackson]

Melksham station in Wiltshire on 6 June 1962 with the evening 'stopper' from Swindon to Westbury headed by No.4948 *Northwick Hall.* A term frowned on by some railway enthusiasts, who preferred the more correct 'stopping train', this was nevertheless the engineman's usual name for these all-stations locals.   [T. W. Nicholls]

Two views of the car ferry trains which ran through the Severn Tunnel, loading and unloading at Pilning or Severn Tunnel Junction. 51xx tanks usually worked the service, with two or three bogie or other flat wagons and a single composite coach making up the train. The scene above is at Pilning in July 1958 and the one below at the other 'terminus' in April 1965—a date just prior to the cessation of these trains as a result of the opening of the new suspension bridge across the estuary.

[H. C. Casserley, B. D. Coldwell]

The activity at a large station in steam days was always made to seem more busy than it actually was by the unceasing to-and-fro movements of a station pilot or two—adding a coach on to a train, perhaps removing a couple of vans from a waiting parcels train, remarshalling empty stock, etc, etc. This is the East End pilot at Bristol (Temple Meads) on 6 March 1960, 2-6-2T No.5561 from Bath Road shed.

[M. J. Jackson]

No.4902 *Aldenham Hall* near Bathampton with an up local consisting of five coaches and loaded milk tanks, July 1953.

[J. C. Hillmer]

With twenty or more wagons leaning on her bunker down the 1 in 100 run westward through Box Tunnel, Pannier No.8738 is rattling along quite fast enough for her driver's peace of mind.... This pick-up freight was photographed in this classic GWR setting in July 1953.

[J. C. Hillmer]

Looking very smart at the head of twelve chocolate-and-cream liveried coaches, No.6028 *King George VI* has paused at the west end of Newton Abbot station to uncouple its pilot and now re-starts the up 'Limited'; 14 September 1957.   [T. E. Williams]

Another station pilot; 2-6-2T No.4174 at the East end of Newton Abbot station, 30 July 1959.   [P. H. Hanson]

2-8-0 No.4703 with the 4.10 p.m. Kingswear-Taunton approaching Oyster Bend Bridge beside the South Devon Coast on 10 September 1962.   [J. R. Besley]

Two views of No.4704 at Newton Abbot on 14 July 1961, with the 10.20 a.m. Paignton-Plymouth. This train reverses here and No.4704 has just taken over (above). Below, departing from No.6 platform (normally used by up trains) with a group of youthful spotters running alongside.   [J. R. Besley]

CENTLEMEN
ADIES
WAITING ROOM
REFRESHMENTS
6
4704
4
NEWTON ABBOT

6
6
4704

2-6-2T No.4555 passing Lustleigh on the daily Moretonhampstead-Newton Abbot goods, 13 March 1961. By this date, the branch was closed to pasengers although the station nameboard still survived among the weeds.

[J. R. Besley]

No.6940 *Didlington Hall* at Kingskerswell, near Aller Junction, with an afternoon Paignton-Paddington express in April 1961.

[W. L. Underhay]

Running bunker-first, 2-6-2T No.6146 rounds the curve through the cutting near Noss Shipyard on what is now the Torbay & Dartmouth Railway, on 7 August 1961. The train is the 3.55 p.m. from Exeter, destined for Kingswear. [W. L. Underhay]

'Liskeard, change for Looe.' No.4922 *Enville Hall* runs in underneath the road bridge which spans the station, heading an up Birmingham relief in May 1959. As can be seen, the line falls sharply past the goods shed and sidings, at 1 in 59 down a reverse curve onto Moorswater Viaduct.   [M. Mensing]

A train from off the Perranporth and Newquay branch, which at one time joined the main line at Chacewater, draws into Truro station in September 1959 behind a 41xx tank. The Falmouth branch trains used the bay on the extreme left.

[P. Q. Treloar]

No.5097 *Sarum Castle,* on a lengthy Penzance-Crewe parcels, has just crossed Angarrack viaduct in west Cornwall and is on the 1 in 61 climb to Gwinear Road. Below No.4089 *Donnington Castle* nears the same location with an up express later that day. The milepost by the locomotive records the 317½ miles to Paddington over the route via Temple Meads and Bath.

[P. Q. Treloar]

Over the demanding and hilly Cornish main line, which called for sheer power rather than any sustained speed, the 'Counties' were good machines and always gave a good account of themselves. This is No.1002 *County of Berks,* at grips with the sharp (1 in 67) pull away from St. Erth—one which faced westbound trains immediately after the stop there for St. Ives-bound passengers. Her train is composed of twelve coaches, originating in Birmingham and worked by No.1002 from Temple Meads.

[P. Q. Treloar]